AN APPALACHIAN CHILDHOOD

GROWING UP IN A HOLLER IN THE MOUNTAINS

Karen Gravelle

GROWING UP IN AMERICA

Franklin Watts

A Division of Grolier Publishing
New York London Hong Kong Sydney
Danbury, Connecticut

Cover and interior design by Molly Heron
Map by Joe LeMonnier
Photograph p. 34 © Corbis-Bettman; photographs pp. 17, 23, 24, 26 (bottom), 44, 51, 56,
57 provided to the author; all other photographs © Karen Gravelle.

Library of Congress Cataloging-in-Publication Data

Gravelle, Karen.
Growing up— in a holler in the mountains / by Karen Gravelle.
p.   cm. — (Growing up in America)
Includes bibliographical references and index.

Summary: Presents a description of contemporary life
in the Appalachian Region of Kentucky while focusing on the
home and activities of ten-year-old Joseph Ratliff and his family.

ISBN 0-531-11452-X

1. Appalachian Region, Southern—Social life and customs—
Pictorial works—Juvenile literature. 3. Children—Appalachian Region,
Southern—Social life and customs—Pictorial works—Juvenile literature.
4. Children—Kentucky—Social life and customs—Pictorial works—Juvenile literature.
[1. Appalachian Region, Southern—Social life and customs.
2. Kentucky—Social life and customs. 3. Ratliff. Joseph.] I. Title.
II. Series: Gravelle, Karen. Growing up in America.
F217.A65G73 1997
974—dc21   97-10957
                                                                                                    CIP
                                                                                                    AC

CONTENTS

ACKNOWLEDGMENTS

This book would not have been possible without the help of Joseph Ratliff, his dad Terry, his mom Deb, and his sister, Carlie. They not only welcomed me into their home, introduced me to people in the community, and spent hours helping me understand the history and culture of Stephens Branch and eastern Kentucky, but they also made writing this book a lot of fun.

I'd like to express my appreciation to the principal and teachers of Martin Elementary School for their assistance as well. Finally, I want to thank the people of Appalachia, who value their heritage enough to preserve it and who were so willing to share their thoughts and experiences with me.

K.G.

ABOUT GROWING UP IN AMERICA

In many ways, people in the United States are very similar to one another. We listen to the same music, watch the same movies and television programs, eat the same burgers, French fries, and pizza, and wear the same clothes.

But if you look closer, you'll see that Americans are different from each other too. Not only do we have traits that make each of us a unique individual, but we also have different characteristics that identify us as belonging to a particular cultural, ethnic, religious, or racial group.

Generally, the longer a particular group of people live in this country and interact with other Americans, the more they become like everyone else. Thus, after a few generations, many immigrants retain relatively little of their original cultures.

However, some groups have been in this country for hundreds of years, yet have kept alive the cultures of their ancestors. In most ways, they live just like other Americans. But, at the same time, they have preserved their own special traditions, religious beliefs, music, foods, ways of talking, and sometimes even their own languages.

Some of these groups came from Europe or Africa, while others are Native Americans who have been here all along. But all have made important contributions to the way Americans live and to the common culture that we share.

I thought you might like to meet some children from these different cultures and learn about their lives, so I decided to write this series to introduce them to you. To begin, I chose a group from the southeastern United States, the part of the country where I grew up. The people who live in the Appalachian Mountains of the South have a special culture of their own. So, I went to the mountains of Kentucky to see if I could find a child who would tell you what growing up in Appalachia is like.

I thought a good place to start would be at "Seedtime on the Cumberland," a festival held each year in Whitesburg, Kentucky, to celebrate Appalachian culture. There I met Terry Ratliff, a furniture maker who demonstrates traditional woodworking techniques at the festival. He introduced me to his son, Joseph.

Joseph thought a book about Appalachia was a very good idea! He invited me to come to his house, so that I could show you what life is like for him and his friends in Stephens Branch, Kentucky.

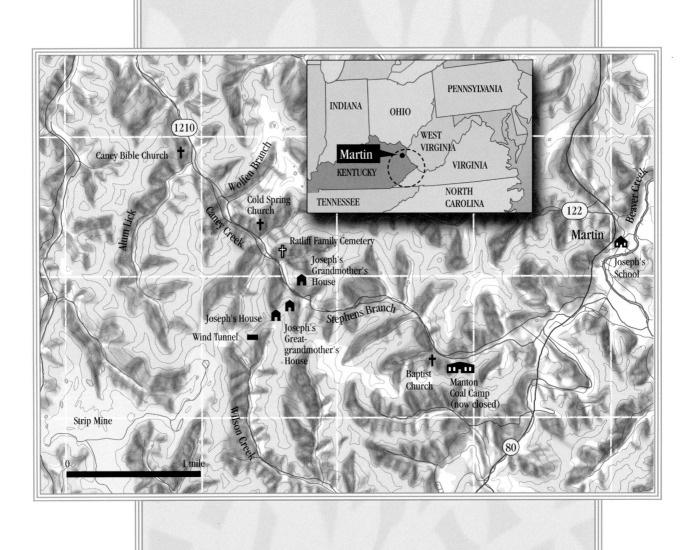

Caney Bible Church †

1210

Wolfen Branch

Alum Lick

Caney Creek

Cold Spring Church †

Ratliff Family Cemetery †

Joseph's Grandmother's House

Joseph's House

Wind Tunnel

Joseph's Great-grandmother's House

Stephens Branch

Wilson Creek

Strip Mine

0   1 mile

INDIANA

OHIO

PENNSYLVANIA

WEST VIRGINIA

Martin

KENTUCKY

VIRGINIA

TENNESSEE

NORTH CAROLINA

122

Martin

Beaver Creek

Joseph's School

Baptist Church †

Manton Coal Camp (now closed)

80

WHERE—AND WHAT—IS APPALACHIA?

The Appalachian Mountains stretch almost 2,000 miles (3,219 km) from Newfoundland in the north to central Alabama in the south. But when people talk about Appalachia and Appalachian people, they usually mean the southern Appalachian Mountains and the folks who live there. People in this region pronounce Appalachia as if they were saying, "I'm going to throw an *apple at ya*."

The area considered to have the most distinctive Appalachian culture is the coal-mining region where southern West Virginia, southwestern Virginia, and eastern Kentucky all come together. This is where Joseph and his family live.

JOSEPH'S STORY

In the late 1700s, settlers of **Scots-Irish**, German, and English descent began to flood into the southern Appalachian Mountains from earlier settlements, looking for land. Among them was William Reilly Ratliff, the great-great-great grandfather of ten-year-old Joseph Ratliff. "He came through Pound Gap from Virginia," Joseph says, "to right here."

"Right here" is a hollow in the mountains of eastern Kentucky called Stephens Branch. A hollow, pronounced "holler" by people in Appalachia, is a narrow little valley with a creek running along the bottom of it. Joseph's house is on a ridge at the end of Stephens Branch. Just past his house, the road drops into Caney and Alum Lick, two other hollows. Joseph's family has lived in these three hollows for two hundred years.

Joseph and his dog, Buddy, have explored most of the ridge behind his house.

There are many reasons why they've stayed here so long. Like most people in Appalachia, Joseph loves the mountains that surround him. Besides being beautiful, they provide lots of things to do. For example, Joseph likes to take his dog, Buddy, and explore the woods behind his house.

One of their favorite places is a cave on the side of the mountain. "The wind carved out the sandstone here, and made a tunnel," Joseph explains. The cave is big enough to sleep several adults, but few people besides Joseph know where it is. He uses it for shelter when it rains, or as a place to be by himself.

Joseph's neighborhood is a pretty safe place for kids. Although there are no street lights in Stephens Branch, he's used to finding his way home from friends' houses in the dark. Joseph's parents make him take a flashlight because there may be poisonous copperhead snakes around. But other than that, there's little reason to worry about him.

When it starts to rain, Joseph keeps warm and dry by building a fire in the wind cave.

Joseph and his family live in the log part of the house. Below is his father's woodworking studio, his mother's office, and a large family room for watching TV.

LIVING IN A DOGTROT HOUSE

Joseph's father built the house where Joseph and his family live. In many ways, their home is very modern. There's a microwave, a television with Nintendo games, cellular phones, and a computer in the basement, where Joseph's mother works. But, except for a new bathroom and kitchen, its structure is very similar to that of the cabins of early pioneers.

Houses like Joseph's home are called dogtrot cabins because of their design. A dogtrot cabin is really two separate cabins built a few feet apart. A single roof covers both cabins, joining them together to make one house. In the 1800s and early 1900s, the space between the two cabins was often left open on both ends. Because the family dogs used this corridor to go from the front yard to the backyard, these homes were called dogtrot cabins.

In Joseph's house, the cabin on the right is made up of two bedrooms, one for him and the other for his sister. Joseph's parents sleep in a large loft on top of these two rooms. The kitchen and living room are in the cabin on the left.

The dogtrot space in between is closed off by a door at the front and by the bathroom at the back. In the past, people built a fireplace between the two cabins to heat both sides of the house, but Joseph's family has a wood-burning stove there instead.

Joseph's father used an old traditional skill to decide where to drill the well to provide water for the house. Since it's difficult and expensive to drill a well, he wanted to pick a place where he was sure to find water. First, he cut a forked twig from a willow or a peach tree. Then, holding the two ends of the fork, one in each hand, he walked around the area where the house was to be built. When the pointed end of the stick dipped down, he knew there was water underground.

In Kentucky, this practice is known as **witching a well.** In other parts of the country, it's sometimes called water witching or dowsing. Only a few people have the special ability to witch a well. Like other talents, it's considered a gift.

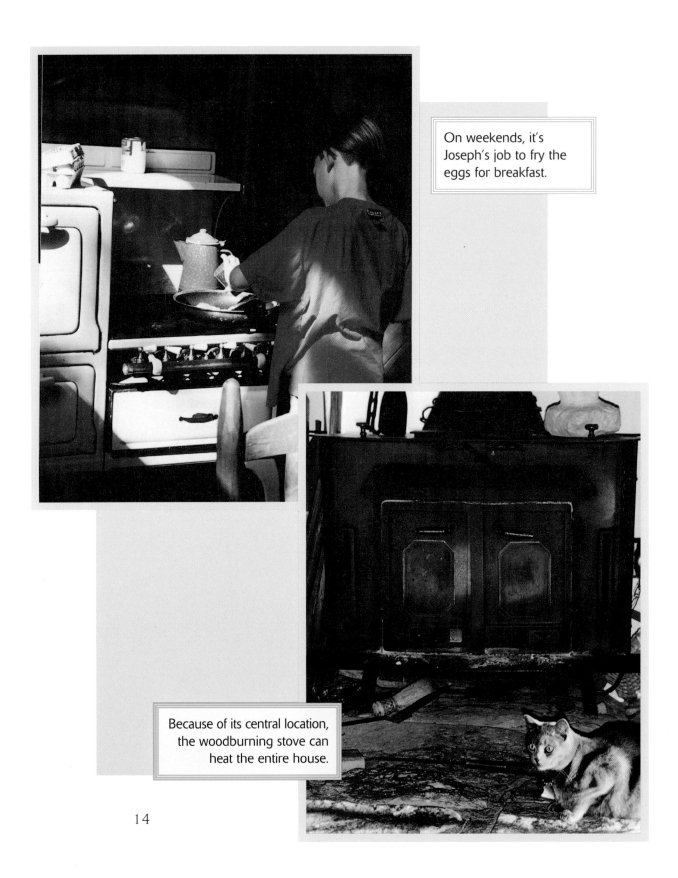

On weekends, it's Joseph's job to fry the eggs for breakfast.

Because of its central location, the woodburning stove can heat the entire house.

14

Another good thing about living in Stephens Branch is that there are plenty of relatives around. Joseph's grandmother lives just across the road. And next to Joseph's house, at the bottom of the hill, is his great-grandmother's home.

Because hollows are small, with few people, some children in the mountains of Kentucky play mostly with their own cousins and brothers and sisters. Joseph's best friend, J. P., lives across the road and isn't related to him. But Joseph and his fourteen-year-old sister, Carlie, are very close and enjoy each other's company.

Joseph and Carlie have to get up early each morning to get to school on time. Carlie is in high school now, but Joseph attends elementary school in Martin, a town of about eight hundred people. His teachers know his family very well. They had his sister in their classes a few years ago, and his father also attended the school as a boy.

Joseph and his sister, Carlie, try to see how high they can jump.

When doing math problems, the students in Joseph's class work in pairs.

Joseph's favorite subject is science.

Joseph isn't sure what he'd like to study when he gets older, nor what he wants to be when he grows up, but if he's like many people in eastern Kentucky, he'll probably earn his living from a combination of activities.

The earliest white settlers of Appalachia were people who cherished their independence and were used to relying on themselves. In many ways, their descendants still have that spirit of independence and self-reliance. Like their ancestors, they are resourceful in finding ways to earn a living. Since there is little flat farm land, even farmers have to do other things beside growing crops and raising livestock. Most farmers need several sources of income.

Joseph may decide to follow in his dad's footsteps. Joseph's father is one of many Appalachian people who enjoy working on their own. After graduating from college, he was employed as a psychologist, helping people deal with

Farms in the hollows of Appalachia are small because there isn't a lot of flat land.

They look like leather strips, but these are actually strips of hickory bark that Joseph's father uses in making chairs. Next to them are baskets made of white oak.

their emotional and social problems. But his real love was woodworking, and he now makes chairs, tables, and other items from the trees in Stephens Branch. Some of his wood-working knowledge was learned from other craftspeople, but he picked up many skills on his own. His talent at using old-fashioned techniques and the beauty of the things he produces make his furniture very valuable. Joseph's dad exhibits his work in arts and crafts shows as far away as Connecticut. People from all over the country see his work at these shows and order chairs and tables from him.

Some of the chairs Joseph's dad makes are put together without any nails, pegs, or glue. Chairs like this are constructed from newly cut wood that has not dried yet. When the wood dries, it shrinks, locking the joints tightly in place. The seat of the chair is woven from strips of tree bark. "Those seats can last a hundred years," his father says.

Joseph's father used several different types of wood in making this chair. The frame is mulberry and osage orange; the seat and back are woven out of hickory bark.

Joseph is learning a lot about woodworking from his dad. "To start, you have to know the different kinds of trees to use for different parts of a chair," Joseph explains. Sometimes, Joseph goes with his father to pick the trees for a piece of furniture. Often, they get wood from their own property. But since many people in the area know that Joseph's dad is a furniture maker, they offer him trees that have fallen or been blown down in a storm. Joseph already has some projects of his own that his dad is helping him with.

Joseph's mother works for an insurance company. She has an office in the basement, right next to his father's woodworking shop. She chose this job in part because she wanted to be at home while Joseph and his sister were growing up.

Besides the income from his parents' jobs, Joseph's family raises some livestock. In fact, the family's pets and farm animals outnumber the people. In addition to two **hound dogs,** Buddy and Trixie, a cat named Smokey, and a parakeet, the Ratliffs have two

When Joseph gets into difficulty with his woodworking projects, his father helps him.

roosters and five hens. They used to have a pig, Sam, that they got as a piglet. But, when Sam reached 300 pounds (136 kg), broke into the basement, and ate all the food stored there, he lost his position as a pet and became food himself.

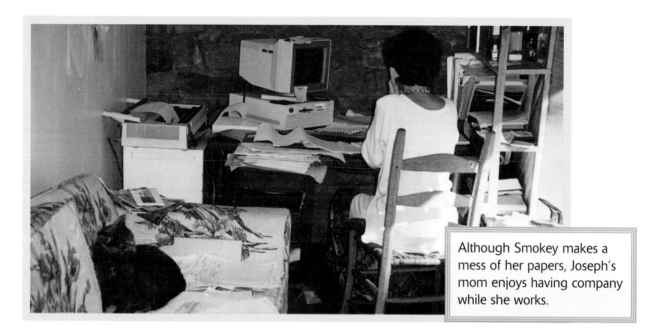

Although Smokey makes a mess of her papers, Joseph's mom enjoys having company while she works.

TOMBSTONES IN THE WELL

Storytelling is an important activity in Appalachia. Sometimes the stories folks tell are **tall tales.** These are just for fun and aren't meant to be believed. But the ones people like best are true stories of things that happened in their own towns and hollows, to their ancestors and their neighbors' ancestors. These stories are passed down from generation to generation.

One of Joseph's favorite stories is about a family who lived in Stephens Branch in the 1860s during the **Civil War**. As Joseph's father tells it, "The War was devastating for people here. One hollow would take up with the north, the Union side, while the next hollow might be for the Confederacy. Even families were divided. A lot of folks thought both sides were equally bad. Armies would come in, gather up the young men to fight with them, steal all the corn, horses, and cattle, and move back out.

"Law and order broke down completely. Bands of roving men who weren't on either side would ride in and raid farms, just take what they wanted. Sometimes, in all the turmoil, families had whole farms stolen from them. That's what happened to the Kennedys, just down the road here.

"The Kennedys had a good-sized place. Old man Kennedy was dying, and this other fellow figured this was a chance to steal their land. He made up a fake **deed** and signed the old man's name, thinking that no one would be able to prove it was forged once the old man was dead. Then he took the deed to the courthouse and got it filed. In the middle of all this, the old man passed away.

"But it seems the fellow made a little mistake. People got to looking at the date on the tombstone and saw that old Kennedy had died two days before the date on the deed, so he couldn't have signed it. Now the fellow knew he was in trouble. He hired some men to throw the tombstone down a well, so there wouldn't be any evidence of what he'd done. That well is 60 feet deep, so there was no way of hauling that tombstone back up. Far as I know, it's still there today."

People in Stephens Branch find a variety of ways to add to their income. One way of earning money is by digging up ginseng in the woods. Ginseng is a root that is used in tonics and medicines. People keep some for themselves and sell the rest. Hunting dogs are always in demand, so those with good dogs breed them and sell the puppies.

There's always a market for little animals like puppies or baby goats.

A less common practice is to raise fighting cocks. Cockfighting as a sport is legal in only a few states, but raising special fighting roosters is permitted in many parts of the country, including Kentucky. Good birds bring a high price, and people come from as far away as the Philippines to buy them.

The Appalachian mountains are rich in timber, and many people allow parts of their land to be **logged.** Joseph has no objection to this, but he definitely doesn't like to see whole hillsides completely stripped of trees. "They should take only the trees they want," he says, "instead of cutting them all down and ruining everything." Since removing all the trees from an area leads to soil **erosion,** this practice can cause serious problems.

Fighting cocks are very aggressive, so they must be raised in separate pens to keep them from attacking each other.

The most important natural resources of the Appalachian area have been its coal and timber. When northern coal companies came into the mountains in the late 1800s, they completely changed life in the region. Coal mining is hard and dangerous work, and miners work for a company, not themselves. Therefore, many of the Appalachian men who owned land preferred working on their farms rather than going into the mines. Also, some company operators thought that the mountain people were too independent to make good employees. Thus, in order to get enough miners, the companies brought in thousands of workers from other parts of the United States and from Europe. Then they built whole towns for them to live in.

The Appalachian Mountains are rich in timber resources.

Joseph hates to see the hillsides stripped of trees. "This place always makes me sad," he says.

Many of the trees logged in the area are cut into boards at a small local sawmill.

26

THE PEOPLE OF APPALACHIA

The earliest inhabitants of the southern Appalachian Mountains were the Cherokee, a nation of twenty-five thousand people who lived in parts of present-day Virginia, North Carolina, South Carolina, Kentucky, Tennessee, Georgia, and Alabama.

The first European explorer, Hernando de Soto, entered the mountains of Tennessee in 1580. However, whites did not attempt to colonize the southern Appalachians until about 150 years later. Then, toward the middle of the 1700s, German and Scots-Irish settlers began to move into the mountains from Pennsylvania, traveling down the Shenandoah and other valleys. By 1800, they were joined by settlers from eastern Virginia and North Carolina who crossed into Kentucky through the mountain gaps near Cumberland. Most of these people, including Joseph's ancestors, were of English and Scots-Irish descent.

The settlers slowly took over the land of the Cherokee. Many Indians died of diseases the settlers brought with them, while others were killed outright by the newcomers. Still other Cherokee people married settlers and were absorbed into the white population. Like many whites who have lived in Appalachia for centuries, Joseph's family has a small amount of Cherokee blood.

In 1837, the United States government drove the remaining Cherokee out, forcing them to move across the Mississippi River. However, a handful escaped by taking refuge in the mountains. Over ten thousand of their descendants now live on the Cherokee reservation in western North Carolina.

Before the Civil War, slavery was legal in the southern Appalachians. But since the land was too mountainous for large plantations, few landowners had slaves. As a result, the African-American population was small. This changed in the early 1900s, when northern industrialists began to develop the mineral resources of Appalachia. Coal companies brought in new groups of people—including African Americans and Eastern Europeans—to work in the mines. Although most of these people left when the mines started to close in the 1940s and 1950s, some remained.

Appalachians are now a mix of people with Native American, Scots-Irish, English, German, Eastern European, African, and other backgrounds. By far the largest number of people, however, are of Scots-Irish descent, and their influence is felt throughout Appalachia.

"There was a coal camp right here in Stephens Branch," Joseph's father says. "Over two thousand people lived there. It had two boarding houses, police officers, three-story buildings, and a place called Silk Stocking Row, where the company officials lived, right next to the company store."

Like most people in the coal-mining areas of Appalachia, Joseph's family was both helped and hurt by the mines. Despite the dangerous and difficult work, the added income from

Southwestern Virginia, eastern Kentucky, and southern West Virginia still have vast amounts of coal. This exposed coal seam is right next to the road running through Stephens Branch.

mining jobs brought in much-needed cash and resulted in a big improvement in the standard of living, so more and more Appalachian men went to work in the mines. For example, by working eight to ten hours in the mines and then farming when he got home, Joseph's great-grandfather was able to buy the land Joseph's family lives on now. The coal companies also built many roads and bridges, making it easier for people to get around.

But the mining industry brought problems too. Working conditions in the mines were unsafe, and the coal companies were not interested in the well-being of the miners. As Joseph's father recalls, "The attitude of the owners was, 'You're driving this mule and you're hauling the coal out of that mine. Now, if the top starts to fall in, you be sure you get my mule out of the mine! If your buddies are back there and you can get them out, that's OK. But make sure that mule gets out—I'll need it in the morning.'"

CEMETERIES

In the mountains of eastern Kentucky, many families have their own small cemeteries. Usually, these cemeteries are near the house or in a pretty spot in another part of the property.

Joseph's family has a little cemetery on a hill just down the road. It's up to Joseph and his father to keep the grass mowed and take care of things, so Joseph is there frequently. The oldest grave in the cemetery is that of Joseph's

The tradition of building a roof over the grave originated before the 1800s in the British Isles.

The Ratliff family cemetery is on a little hill by the side of the road.

great-great-grandmother, Nancy Ratliff, who was born at the beginning of the Civil War.

Some of the graves in these mountain cemeteries are unusual. Occasionally, people build a wooden shelter over the grave, as their ancestors did long ago in the British Isles. Although this custom has died out in Europe, it is still practiced in a few places in Appalachia. Joseph's cousins, who also live in Stephens Branch, have a grave like this in their cemetery.

Many miners developed a disease called **black lung** from years of working in coal dust. This disease is very serious, making it difficult to breathe, much less work, and there is no cure for it. Yet, if the miners became sick, the company did not give them a **pension**, so many were left unable to work and without an income.

Joseph's grandfather suffered from black lung, so Joseph knows how bad this disease is. "Pa used to cough until he turned blue," Joseph says, remembering his grandfather's struggle to breathe.

To get the coal companies to improve working conditions and to pay decent benefits and salaries, the miners organized into **unions**. The unions called for the miners to strike, or stop working. By forcing the mines to close down, the unions hoped to make the coal companies change their practices. But the companies tried to keep the mines open by bringing in new workers who weren't part of the union. Union members called these workers **scabs** and had great contempt for them.

The coal strikes of the 1910s, 1920s, and 1930s were long and very bitter. But the union finally got the mining companies to agree to provide important benefits for the miners.

WOMEN IN THE MINES

Although women were not allowed to work in the mines, they played important roles in the coal-field strikes that rocked Appalachia in the early 1900s. Some women wrote songs supporting the strikers, such as a famous labor classic, "Which Side Are You On?" Others laid down in front of coal trucks in an effort to close scab (nonunionized) mining operations. Some women fought alongside their husbands in gun battles between miners and the company owners.

The most famous woman involved in the strikes was Mary, or "Mother," Jones. Mother Jones was born in Cork, Ireland, in 1830, and emigrated to the United States. In 1867, her husband and her children died in a yellow-fever epidemic in Memphis, and, four years later, she lost all her possessions in the Chicago Fire of 1871. She then dedicated herself to the labor movement and began to travel the country organizing unions. Because of her courage in the face of danger and her untiring efforts on behalf of miners from West Virginia to Colorado, Mother Jones became a hero in the mining communities of Appalachia.

Mother Jones

In eastern Kentucky, stories of Mother Jones are still told today. "She would go right into these scab operating mines," Joseph's father says, "figuring the company thugs wouldn't shoot her because she was a woman. Now, that was true back then—you just didn't shoot a woman. But if a man had done the things she did, he would have been killed."

The efforts of Mother Jones and men and women like her paid off. In 1933, the mines were finally unionized. In the 1970s, women began to enter the mines as miners. Today, they work alongside men, bringing out coal.

Joseph's family was very active in the miners' union. His grandfather was an officer in the United Mine Workers of America and was right in the middle of the conflict between the union and the coal companies. Things had quieted down somewhat by the 1960s, but Joseph's dad can still remember helping to carry soup to strikers in those years.

"It was during the winter of 1962-63. I was young, only eight years old," his father recalls. "And I'd never seen so many people. There were folks lined up for a long way to get this hot vegetable soup."

His father remembers how determined the strikers were to keep the coal mines closed until a settlement was reached. "The women got out there and laid down in front of the coal trucks to stop the scab mining," he says. "Some of the men shot out the engines of coal trucks with high-powered rifles. No question about it—that coal stayed right where it was!"

The union struggle was successful. It led to better working conditions, higher pay, retirement benefits, and black lung disease benefits. Joseph's grandfather was one of those who received the black lung disease benefits the union had won.

APPALACHIAN CHURCHES

Church-going is a very important part of Appalachian life, as can be seen from the large number of churches in each community. For example, there are three churches in Caney and Stephens Branch alone.

Mountain churches are often different from churches in other parts of the country. For the people of Appalachia, independence and personal freedom have always been important, and these values can be seen in the way they practice religion. Although large denominations, such as the Methodists and Southern Baptists, are found throughout Appalachia, particularly in large towns and broad valleys, many mountain churches are small, independent organizations.

Members of these churches strive for a tender heart that is open to the spirit of God, and religious services are often emotional. Baptism is performed outdoors in a river or creek, and in some churches the old custom of **footwashing** (washing each other's feet to demonstrate humility) is still practiced. Members of most mountain churches take part in yearly revival meetings as well. Although people usually worship in their own home churches, they also enjoy frequent **fellowshipping,** or attending services at neighboring churches.

Many of these churches are found only in Appalachia, and include Old Regular Baptists, Primitive Baptists, Free Will Baptists, Missionary Baptists, Jesus Only (or Oneness), Holiness (independent), Church of God (independent), and Pentecostal Church of God (independent).

Caney Bible Chapel, where Joseph and Carlie went to Bible school, is one of three churches in Stephens Branch and Caney.

In the 1940s, many coal mines began to shut down or to lay off most of their workers. Machinery had been invented that could do work previously performed by human workers, so there was much less need for miners. Most of the people brought in by the coal companies—along with many whose families had been in Appalachia for generations—left the mountains to find work in the cities of the Midwest. Today, there is no trace of Manton, the coal camp of 2,200 people that once occupied the entire lower end of Stephens Branch.

When the mines closed, Joseph's grandparents moved to Indiana to find jobs, taking their children with them. Although the family did well there, Joseph's grandparents and his father returned to Stephens Branch after ten years. Other people also left for a time and then moved back, and a slow stream of newcomers has been trickling into the area too. Joseph's mother is one of these "new" settlers. Originally from Ohio, she moved to nearby Pikeville in the 1970s. Two of Joseph's aunts remained in Indiana and his mother still has relatives in Ohio, so there is a lot of visiting back and forth between Joseph and his cousins in the Midwest.

Despite all the changes over the last one hundred years, many things in eastern Kentucky have remained the same. For example, Appalachian men still go hunting in some of the same places where Daniel Boone tracked buffalo and deer two hundred years ago. This famous pioneer explorer and woodsman spent the winter just a few miles from Stephens Branch, and people in Joseph's community still admire him for his wilderness skills. Like Boone, they value this knowledge and try to pass on their own understanding of the forest and its animals to their children. This is one reason why hunting remains a popular activity in Appalachia.

FOX HUNTING

When men in the hollows of Kentucky hunt, it's usually in part to provide food for their families. But when they go fox hunting, the men leave their guns at home. That's because they aren't interested in catching the fox.

It's easiest for dogs to track a scent when the ground is wet, so the best time for a fox hunt is after it has rained. At dusk, when the weather has cleared, the men and their dogs set out. The men build a campfire, where they'll spend the night talking and listening for their dogs.

The dogs are then let loose. As soon as they catch the scent of a fox, they take off after it, sometimes chasing the

Trixie is the Ratliffs' hunting dog. Unlike Buddy, she has to be tied up most of the time, or she'd run off to go hunting by herself and might not come back.

fox for many miles. Even though they can't see their dogs, the men can tell where they are by the sound of their barking. Since each man knows his own dog's bark, they can also tell which dog is leading the pack. Owning a good hunting dog is very important in Appalachia, and the men take great pride in having a dog in the lead. In fact, finding out who has the best dog is the point of a fox hunt.

The dogs rarely get closer to the fox than a quarter of a mile, but they may chase it for up to fourteen hours. Finally, the fox escapes into its burrow or the dogs just give up. Tired and happy, the men and dogs return home. And the fox can relax for a while.

"Hunting's an opportunity to provide something special for the table," Joseph's dad says. "But, more than that, it's a chance for me to teach Carlie and Joseph the wilderness knowledge that was passed down to me—like what the different trees produce and how that's related to the wildlife."

One thing that Joseph has already learned is that deer can be found near white oak trees. "They like to eat the acorns," he explains.

Although most hunters in Kentucky use regular rifles, Joseph's dad hunts with an old-fashioned **muzzle-loader**, **cap** and **ball** gun. These guns must be reloaded each time they are fired. That takes time—enough for an animal to get away. Thus, a hunter who misses with the first shot usually doesn't get a second chance.

Joseph watches his father carefully to learn how to load a gun correctly.

In addition, old-fashioned guns such as these must be carefully loaded. "If the ball isn't pressed completely down, the gun can explode when you fire it," Joseph says. Joseph's dad is teaching him how to use a gun properly. In target practice with his father and other men, Joseph hits the bull's-eye as often as the adults do. Still, he knows it will be a while before he's ready to go hunting.

Like most people in Stephens Branch, Joseph's family has a garden where they raise tomatoes, peas, corn, beans, lettuce, and beets. His parents could buy their vegetables from the grocery store, but fresh produce from their own yard tastes much better. And, by teaching Joseph and Carlie how to grow and preserve food, their parents are making sure that these skills remain alive.

Because putting information into rhymes makes it easier for children to remember, much of this old-time knowledge is traditionally passed down in short poems. For example, "If you want to end up with one plant," Joseph says, "you have to sow four seeds—'One for the squirrel, one for the crow, one for the ground, and one to grow.'"

At first, Joseph and Carlie weren't too interested in learning to raise their own vegetables. "They didn't understand why we were going to all this trouble," Joseph's mom says. "They griped a lot last year about having to do all that hard work. But now that they get what it's about, they're looking forward to it."

Many people in the Appalachian Mountains still do traditional crafts. At ninety-one years of age, Joseph's great-grandmother continues to sew beautiful quilts. She's lost count of how many she's made over the years, but she knows it's more than one hundred. Most of these were completely hand-stitched, although she occasionally uses a sewing machine on some now.

Other folks make brooms by hand, or weave baskets from strips of white oak. Many people make beautiful baskets; however, the real masters of this art are the Cherokee Indians in North Carolina.

Since many of these traditional skills have been lost in other parts of the country, craft products such as those made in Kentucky have increased in value. In the town of David, about six miles from Stephens Branch, a **cooperative** has been established to help people sell their craft work. The co-op carries quilts, pillows, toys, dolls, baskets, paintings, walking sticks, and many other things. People work at their own level, so everyone from highly skilled artists to elderly people with failing eyesight or arthritis are able to contribute. By joining

Joseph's great-grandmother sits in her living room, surrounded by some of the many quilts she's sewed. She is now making a quilt in the "postage stamp" design (right). Sewing these tiny pieces together takes a long time, and she's been working on this quilt for many years.

Baskets and brooms are some of the other crafts produced by Appalachian people.

together, the craftspeople in the cooperative can reach a wider market and get better prices for their work.

Many men in eastern Kentucky like to **whittle**. When it's not too cold, men in Martin gather together on a corner—each with a knife and a small piece of wood—to whittle and talk. Recently, they built a roof over the bench they sit on so they can whittle in greater comfort. Although they often make things, whittling is done as much for pleasure as it is to produce something.

Throughout eastern Kentucky, men whittle to pass the time. The men of Martin meet to hang out and whittle on this protected bench.

People in eastern Kentucky have a long history of making music, and some of Joseph's relatives earn their living as professional musicians. Joseph is learning to play two instruments, the flute and the banjo. He studies flute at school. He likes it, but that wasn't his main reason for choosing this instrument. "My sister took flute before," he says. "So we already had one." A family friend made a banjo for him, and he's learning to play it on his own.

Whether they know it or not, most people in the rest of the nation are familiar with at least one type of Appalachian music. Country, one of the most popular forms of music in the United States today, grew directly from the traditional music of the southern Appalachian Mountains, and many famous country performers have come from the mountains of Kentucky, Tennessee, and Virginia.

Country isn't the only well-known music form that was born in Appalachia. In the 1940s, traditional music from Kentucky, called **bluegrass,** began to gain popularity outside central Appalachia. Instruments such as fiddles, mandolins, and banjos, and the high-pitched vocal style of the singers give bluegrass an old-fashioned sound. Bluegrass spread through the country during the 1950s and 1960s, when folk music became very popular, and it is now played in many places.

Mountain **gospel** is another type of music that can be heard on local radios. Appalachian gospel music is similar in many ways to African-American gospel, but the two sound somewhat different.

Joseph's banjo is made from a cookie tin. When he wants the sound to be louder, he takes the back off the tin.

SHAPE-NOTE SINGING

Shape notes are a simple way of writing music. Instead of indicating a note by key and position on a series of lines and spaces, notes are written in the form of shapes, such as rectangles, triangles, diamonds, and circles. Thus, all the singer has to memorize is the pitch that goes with each shape.

Shape notation began around 1800 in New England as a way to write the melody of hymns. It quickly spread to the rural South. The earliest shape-note system used shapes and the syllables fa, sol, la, and mi for the notes. By the mid-1800s, a seven-shape system using do, re, mi, fa, sol, la, si, was introduced. Both systems are still used today.

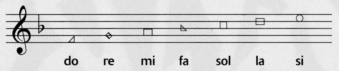

Four-syllable system

fa   sol   la   fa   sol   la   mi

Seven-syllable system

do   re   mi   fa   sol   la   si

Shape-note singing has a very distinctive sound. It's hard to capture this sound in words, but most people agree that shape-note singing has a haunting beauty.

Although shape-note singing has died out in other parts of the country, it is still practiced in some churches in

Appalachia and the deep South. Shape-note conventions, or all-day singings, are held throughout rural communities in these areas. Soloists, trios, and quartets perform, but most of the singing is done by everyone in attendance. At the beginning of each hymn, the melody is sung through once using the fa sol la mi syllables (or the do re mi fa sol la si syllables if a seven-note book is being used). Then, after rehearsing the tune, the singers go on to sing the verses.

The people who attend shape-note conventions enjoy socializing as well as singing. They bring food to contribute for dinner, and following a couple of hours of singing, everyone sits down to a table piled high with good country cooking.

Many Appalachian musicians still play and sing the traditional music of early Scots-Irish settlers. The bagpipes of Ireland and Scotland are missing in Appalachian music, but except for that, it's hard to tell the difference between the traditional music played by today's Appalachian musicians and the traditional music now performed in Ireland and Scotland.

Country, bluegrass, gospel, and traditional music aren't the only kinds of music Joseph and his friends listen to. Like kids throughout the country, they watch MTV and dance to rock music. Joseph prefers heavy metal to other types of music. "My favorite group right now is Nine-Inch Nails," he says.

Music is a big part of the Slone Mountain Squirrel Festival, held each year on a mountain top near Sizemore, Kentucky. "It

A group of traditional musicians warm up before the start of Seedtime, a yearly festival in Whitesburg, Kentucky.

started out as the Slone family reunion," Joseph explains. "But it kept getting bigger and bigger. Now people from all over the county come." Rock bands, gospel groups, country singers, and bluegrass musicians all play under pavilions at the top of the ridge.

The festival was named for the food originally served—squirrel fixed in a variety of ways. But for those who didn't like fried squirrel, squirrel gravy, or big pots of squirrel stew, there was venison, alligator tail, and groundhog. The festival has gotten much bigger now, and most people bring their own picnic lunches.

For kids Joseph's age, the contests are the best part of the festival. There's horseshoe tossing, three-legged races, and sack races, with prizes for the winners. There's also a greased pole with money tied at the top. The first one to shinny up the pole gets the money.

"But the most fun is the greased pig chase!" Joseph says. Actually, there are several pig chases—one for young girls, another for young boys, and a third for older boys.

"Sometimes there are as many as 150 kids in a big circle," Joseph's father says. "They put this little pig coated with grease in the middle, and yell, 'Go!' The kids mob the pig, all trying to grab it."

"It's kind of like trying to hold on to a greased football," he adds. "The pig keeps squirting out of your arms, squealing like mad. In past years, some of the pigs have gotten away. They just disappeared over the hill with the kids chasing them."

One of the pigs that didn't escape was Sam. Carlie caught him in the Squirrel Festival pig chase when she was nine years old. "She was very proud of herself," Joseph's mother recalls, "but poor Sammy was scared to death. He squealed all the way home."

Sam was this size when the Ratliffs brought the piglet home.

MOUNTAIN COOKING

Like kids in the rest of the country, Joseph and his friends enjoy hamburgers, pizza, soft drinks, hot dogs, French fries, and milk shakes. But some of their favorite things are traditional mountain foods. Church dinners are a great place to find this kind of cooking. Here's what might be on the table at an Old Regular Baptist church dinner.

Chicken and dumplings
Fried chicken
Ham
Mashed potatoes
Pickled vegetables (sauerkraut, pickled corn, pickled beans)
Green beans
Soup beans (pinto beans cooked with salt bacon)
Shuck beans (dried green beans that have been soaked and cooked with bacon)
Greens (collard greens, turnip greens, kale)
Hominy (a dish made from corn kernels)
Cornbread
Blackberry or cherry dumplings
Pies, including fried apple pie
Cakes
Banana pudding

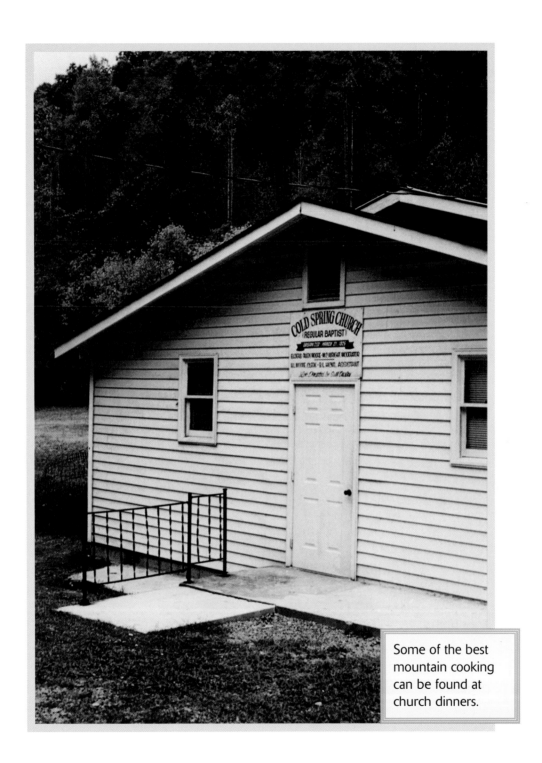

Some of the best mountain cooking can be found at church dinners.

Joseph soars off the side of the mountain on his rope swing. In this position, he's directly over his great-grandmother's house.

In warm weather, it seems as if there's a festival in eastern Kentucky almost every weekend. One of the oldest is the Highlands Folk Festival, when people get together to celebrate the music and traditions of the Irish and Scottish highlands. The festival begins with men in kilts playing bagpipes, but most of the music features traditional mountain instruments such as fiddles, banjos, mandolins, guitars, and dulcimers. In addition to the performers on stage, groups form spontaneously in the parking lot and just start playing.

"Sometimes, guys on the back of a pickup truck are even better than the professionals," Joseph's dad says. "It's really great! You get to hear a lot of old-timers that way."

Besides large festivals, there are singing conventions, church dinners, and other local get-togethers that are a lot of fun.

With so many good things about life in Stephens Branch, it's hard for Joseph to imagine ever leaving. However, when he is a little older, his feelings may change. His sister, Carlie, likes Stephens Branch too, but as a teenager, she's eager to move to a bigger place. With no public transportation in the area, she's stuck at home by herself after school. "You can't hang out with your friends here," she complains. "I'm not old enough to drive yet, and everyone I know lives too far away to walk to."

An important factor in determining whether Joseph stays may be whether or not he can find the kind of job he wants when he grows up. Today, as in the past, many people have to leave eastern Kentucky in order to find work. However, like Joseph's grandparents and his father, some of those who leave come back later.

One thing is sure. Wherever Joseph decides to live as an adult, he'll take very happy memories of Stephens Branch with him.

HOW TYPICAL ARE JOSEPH AND HIS FAMILY?

Some of you may wonder whether Joseph and his family are typical of the people who live in Appalachia. After all, they aren't poor and uneducated, like the Appalachian people you often see on TV and in the movies. But actually, it is these distorted images—not the Ratliff family—that aren't typical.

As one of Joseph's teachers says, "When television crews come down here from New York to do a program on Appalachia, they drive right by the places where the majority of us live, looking for the most poverty-stricken little holler

Since it's hard to hang out with her friends after school, Carlie uses the phone a lot to keep in touch.

around. Then, when they get there, they hunt out the very poorest family they can find. And that's who they take pictures of!" Needless to say, this makes people in Joseph's community very angry.

It is true that there are some very poor people in eastern Kentucky, but there are also some very rich folks. Joseph's family is where most people are—in the middle. And, while his parents may be more educated than some adults in Stephens Branch, they certainly aren't the only college graduates around.

The principal of Martin Elementary School is familiar with every child in the area. In her view, Joseph and his family are very typical of people in the community. And she's in a good position to know!

Someone made these birdhouses and whirligigs just for fun and put them up by the railroad tracks in town.

GLOSSARY

Ball—A small metal ball that is used as a bullet in old-fashioned guns.

Black lung—A disease affecting coal miners; caused by inhaling coal dust. Black spots appear on the lungs and make breathing very difficult.

Bluegrass—A high-pitched type of music associated with the southern Appalachians and played on string instruments, such as the guitar, mandolin, banjo, and fiddle.

Cap—A paper or metal container holding an explosive charge.

Civil War—The war fought in the United States between the northern states, called the Union, and the southern states, called the Confederacy. The war lasted from 1861 until the Confederacy surrendered in 1865.

Cooperative—A business owned and operated by its members. In a cooperative, the profits are shared by the members.

Deed—A document stating the owner of a particular piece of land or a house.

Erosion—The wearing away of the surface of the earth by water or wind.

Fellowshipping—A custom in which members of one church visit other churches to worship.

Footwashing—A custom in which members of a church wash each other's feet as a way of symbolizing humility.

Gospel singing—A type of religious music.

Hound dog—A type of hunting dog that uses its sense of smell to find prey.

Logging—Cutting down trees for lumber.

Muzzle-loader—An old-fashioned gun that is loaded by pushing the ball and explosive charge down the open end of the muzzle.

Pension—Money paid by an employer to a retired or disabled worker.

Scabs—Nonunion workers brought in by companies to replace striking workers.

Scots-Irish—People of Scottish descent who settled in northern Ireland.

Tall tales—Exaggerated stories told for amusement.

Union—An association of workers formed to protect their jobs and improve their working conditions, pay, and benefits.

Witching a well—Locating underground water for a well by using a forked branch; also called dowsing or water witching.

Whittle—To cut or shape something out of a piece of wood by cutting off bits with a knife.

MORE ABOUT APPALACHIA

BOOKS
Picture Books

Ragsale, by Artie Ann Bates (Houghton Mifflin, 1995)

Artie Ann Bates is from Blackey, Kentucky, about 30 miles (48 km) from where Joseph and his family live. In *Ragsale*, she writes about the fun of going to second-hand sales in the mountains of eastern Kentucky. Jeff Chapman-Crane, who painted the pictures for this book, is from Kentucky too.

Mama Is a Miner, by George Ella Lyon (Orchard Books, 1994)

You might not guess it from her first name, but George Ella is a woman. She lives in Lexington, Kentucky, and has written several books about life in the Appalachian Mountains. *Mama Is a Miner* tells what it's like to work in a coal mine. The artist who illustrated the book, Peter Catalanotto, is also familiar with Appalachia—his ancestors worked in the coal mines there.

Appalachia: The Voices of Sleeping Birds, by Cynthia Rylant (Harcourt Brace and Company, 1991)

Both Cynthia Rylant, who wrote this book, and Barry Moser, who painted the pictures, grew up in Appalachia. *Appalachia* is about the lives of mountain folks—and of the dogs that are so important to them.

The Rag Coat, by Lauren Mills (Little, Brown, and Company, 1991)

A quilt coat made from scraps donated by the women of her Appalachian community make it possible for this turn-of-the-century girl to go to school.

Come a Tide, by George Ella Lyon (Orchard Books, 1990)

In this humorous tale, four families on an Appalachian hillside cope with a spring flood that washes away gardens, porches, pigs, and chickens.

The Relatives Came, by Cynthia Rylant (Simon and Schuster, 1985; Aladdin, 1993)

When family members move away, Appalachian people maintain close ties through frequent visits. In *The Relatives Came*, a mountain family from Virginia makes a long trip to see much-missed relatives in another state.

Folk Tales

How Rabbit Tricked Otter, and Other Cherokee Trickster Stories, by Gayle
Ross (HarperCollins, 1994)

The Cherokees were the original inhabitants of the southern Appalachian Mountains, and about ten thousand still live there. This collection of Cherokee tales is written by Gayle Ross, a direct descendant of a chief of the Cherokee nation. The illustrator, Murv Jacob, is of Kentucky-Cherokee descent.

Novels

Borrowed Children, by George Ella Lyon (Orchard Books, 1988)

In the little hollow of Goose Rock, Kentucky, twelve-year-old Amanda takes care of her baby brother, minds her younger sister, and keeps house for her family of eight, while her mother is sick. When invited to spend Christmas in Memphis with her grandparents, she learns a lot she didn't know about her parents, her family, and herself.

M.C. Higgins, the Great, by Virginia Hamilton (Macmillan, 1974, Aladdin, 1993)

In this story about an African-American family in Appalachia, thirteen-year-old M. C. Higgins works to save his family's home from being buried beneath a huge mound of mining rubble. He also fights for his friendship with Ben, a witchy boy whose family M.C.'s parents fear.

Poetry

Knoxville, Tennessee, by Nikki Giovanni (Scholastic, 1994)

An African-American poet describes the joys of summer spent with her family in Kentucky, eating vegetables right from the garden, going to church picnics, and walking in the mountains.

Biography

Daniel Boone: Young Hunter and Teacher, by Augusta Stevenson (Aladdin, 1986)

The famous explorer and woodsman, Daniel Boone, spent the winter a few miles from Stephens Branch. He helped to open Kentucky to white settlement and is still admired in the region for his wilderness skills. This book describes his boyhood on the frontier of Pennsylvania, his teenage years as a hunter, and his later rescue of white settlers from the Indians.

Travel

The Appalachian Trail, by Ronald M. Fisher (National Geographic Society, 1972)

Growing Up in a Holler in the Mountains and the other books mentioned here are about the southern Appalachian Mountains. However, the Appalachian Mountains stretch north all the way to Canada. The National Park Service has established a hiking trial that starts in Springer Mountain, Georgia, and runs 2,015 miles (3,243 km) north to Mount Katahdin, Maine. *The Appalachian Trail* describes the entire mountain range, and the people and animals that live there. There's even a picture of Pound Mountain, Virginia, where Joseph's ancestors crossed into Kentucky almost two hundred years ago.

MOVIES

Although these are old movies, they can often be rented as videos or seen occasionally on television.

Coal Miner's Daughter

This movie traces the life of Loretta Lynn, who came from a poor coal-mining family in Butcher's Hollow, Kentucky, and became one of the most famous country singers of all time.

Matewan

Matewan is based on a 1920 coal miners' strike in Matewan, Kentucky. The strike is also known as the Matewan Massacre and, since this movie is based on facts, it may contain more violence than your parents want you to see. However, if your parents approve, you may want to watch this movie because it will give you a good idea of the terrible conditions coal miners struggled against.

INDEX

African Americans, 28
Appalachia
    burial practices in, 30
    Civil War in, 22, 28, 32
    coal mining in, 25, 28, 30, 32, 37
    defined, 9
    hunting in, 3740
    map, 8
    methods of earning a living in, 17–21, 23–26
    religion in, 35, 36
    settlement of, 17, 27, 28
    traditional cooking in, 50, 52
    traditional crafts in, 41–44
    traditional music in, 45–50, 54
    unions and, 32–35

Baptism, 36. *See also* Religion
Black lung disease, 32. *See also* Coal mining
Bluegrass music, 45, 48. *See also* Music, traditional
Boone, Daniel, 37

Cemeteries, 30
Cherokee Indians, 27, 28, 41
Church dinners, 52
Civil War, 22, 28, 32
Coal mining, 9, 25, 28, 30, 32–35, 37. *See also* Strikes; Unions; Black lung disease
Cockfighting, 24

Cooperative, as outlet for traditional crafts, 41. *See also* traditional crafts.
Copperhead snakes, 11
Country music, 45, 48. *See also* Music, traditional
Crafts, traditional
    basket weaving, 41
    broom making, 41
    quilting, 41
    whittling, 44
    woodworking, 18, 20

Dogtrot cabin, 12, 13
Dowsing, 13

Farming, 17
Fellowshipping. *See* Religion
Foods, traditional, 52. *See also* Church dinners
Footwashing. *See* Religion
Fox hunting, 38, 39

Gardening, 40
Ginseng collecting, 23
Gospel music, mountain, 45, 48. *See also* Music, traditional
Greased pig chase, 50

Highlands Folk Festival, 54
Hollows, 9
Hunting dogs, 20. *See also* Fox hunting
Hunting, 37–40